MANIPULATION

*A Psychologist's Guide to Detect Emotional
Manipulation, Spot Mind Control Tricks of
Influence & Persuasion Tactics to
Defend Against It*

KATHERINE CHAMBERS

TABLE OF CONTENTS

INTRODUCTION

"If you allow people to make more withdrawals than deposits in your life, you will be out of balance and in the negative. Know when to close the account"

(Manipulation)

My life to an outsider might look like it's been all plain sailing and success, it may seem like I have had a perfect upbringing and resulting relationships. However regardless of how great it undoubtedly has been, there have been times where I have had to deal with some rather unsavory situations. Just like everyone else on this planet.

Whilst our civilization at large is predicated on the emotions of love, gratitude and compassion, ultimately our species is still very self-serving. This is not necessarily a bad thing, as we need to take care of ourselves first and foremost in order to look out for the well-being of others around us. But some folks have a tendency to take this too far.

Regardless of how emotionally stable you currently are, human being's have a tendency to act in certain ways and one of those is to be manipulative from time to time. It's inescapable. Fortunately it's usually only for brief spells when we are younger and less consciously aware of what we are doing, nobody is perfect after all.

But the problem comes when people hold onto these traits into their adult life. When they start to use these manipulative tactics in a calculating and intentional fashion to get what they want from the people around them.

I have a habit of breaking these psychological principles down into the simplest of terms and manipulation is no different. In reality dealing with such behavior is about doing two things in life:

1. Understanding the manipulation tactics people use - why they are doing this and who they are most likely to target.

2. Learning the strategies to defend against them - to inoculate yourself from this type of behavior.

So again, whilst having a generally friction free upbringing, I certainly found myself in my fair share of manipulative relationships whilst in college and early adult life. I had a certain friend who would constantly lean on me for help with her course work. She would constantly remind me that I was smarter than her or had a more stable family life and should help her out as a result (with literally nothing in return).

I also had a very manipulative relationship in my late 20's when initially trying to build my consulting business. I would be constantly made to feel guilty about the progress I was making, the hours I was spending to build something for what I thought was "our" future, not just my own.

In reality these situations usually arise from people who are simply not in a place of security and comfort themselves, they try to push their luck a little to get what they want or attempt to hold others back as they fear losing them. Ironically this usually has the opposite effect in what they are trying to achieve.

However there are other cases where people are truly just out for getting what they want, they are calculating and ruthless with their actions with little to no regard for the targets of their manipulation. These are the instances and people you really want to avoid.

Therefore my aim for this book is to discuss the most important aspects when it comes to assessing emotional manipulation as a concept. But more critically, the practical ways in which someone can spot the warning signs and raise their levels of confidence and self-esteem to ultimately immunize themselves against any such behavior going forward.

My Credentials

Before we get into the ins and outs of emotional manipulation it's probably a good idea for me to explain exactly who I am, and why you should even bother listening to me in the first place. Yes I have the undergraduate and master's degree in psychology from Stanford, but my main focus over the past 15 years or so has been on the practical elements of the discipline. I wouldn't ever call myself a "Self-Help Guru" but I do focus much more on the results of these principles in the real world compared to my previous life of studying endless research papers on the academic side of the subject.

I use what I have learnt and observe the behavior and psychological patterns of other successful people in life to pin point exactly what it is they are doing to elicit the results they are achieving. There are common patterns to these people and behaviors if you know how to spot them. Luckily for you even if you don't, I have spent the past 2 decades working this stuff out for you. I have dedicated my 40's to documenting both the rationale behind the most important psychological mindsets as well as the practical advice on how to cultivate the ability to use them to your benefit in the real world.

It all started when I was just a young girl growing up on the east coast, I was a very observant kid. I was the youngest of four in our family which was fine with me as I would get to watch my older sister and brothers in action. Watch for their actions and behaviors, their successes and failures as almost a dry run for what I should be doing.

This continued through high school and into college, I luckily had a very active and ambitious peer group, it's hard not to when you live on the Stanford campus. I played a high level of lacrosse as well as

4

track and field whilst at university so got to view the psychology of team/individual sports as well as in academia.

However it's not since leaving college life and living in the real world that I have really developed a taste for the subjects I once studied. It's all well and good reading the intricacies of psychological theories from the comfort of your dorm room or library, but it's not until you have to put these theories to the test in life in general do you really understand how they work. It's not until you have to make your way in business, within a career, build a family for yourself do you really understand the impact your mindset has to your overall success.

For me that has been building a multi-six figure consulting business and now a family of my own. But I am not here to blow my own horn or preach in anyway, nobody needs that. What I will do is put things into perspective, what I know to be true from the science behind these principles combined with my experience in the real world. I have made many mistakes along the way and will point out these pitfalls for you.

So why am I such an expert on emotional manipulation? As I mentioned, I studied a wide range of topics within the field of psychology and neuroscience whilst at college which formed my base understanding, but I have since picked up many critical skill sets whilst building a family and career of my own. Everything from managing my personal relationships with friends/family to client and employee relationships alike. Everything has been a learning curve and one in which took deep emotional understanding and soul searching at times.

The real world is about problem solving, it's about rapport building with others who can help you along the journey. However sometimes these interactions can go awry, they can fall out of balance and you can start to get taken advantage of if you are not careful. They can start to become manipulative in nature.

So now that you know a little more about me, let's dive in. The following chapters will teach you everything you need to know in order to become proficient at spotting manipulation tactics when they arise. But ultimately provide you with the tools and knowledge on how to avoid such behavior in the future. A lot if of this involves improving your own overall confidence and self-worth to naturally shield against these strategies in any situation.

PART 1

A BASIC UNDERSTANDING OF MANIPULATION PRINCIPLES

CHAPTER 1

EMOTIONAL MANIPULATION EXPLORED

"Everybody has the ability to be manipulative, to be hateful and deceitful"

(Neil Labute)

The foundation of healthy relationships is mutual respect, trust, and security. Every person wants to feel loved unconditionally, appreciated, safe to expose all their vulnerabilities, and accepted for who they are. However, everyone falls short from having ideal relationships because of a lot of factors, that's just life.

One might turn to passive aggressive tactics to express pain or get out of an argument. Another could be telling lies or hurling painful words to others to protect themselves from their own sadness, anger, and pain. These kinds of behavior do not promote a healthy relationship.

But that being said, there are no perfect human being's and no perfect relationships in this world. If one or both people has weak emotional intelligence, it will hard to nurture deeper connections and healthy relationships as a result. I write more extensively on this within my book "Emotional Intelligence: A Psychologists Guide" but the significance of having an overall high E.Q. level with regards to either not displaying manipulative behavior yourself or being subjected to it by others is huge.

Emotional Manipulation

However some people are emotionally manipulative and controlling in their relationships by their very nature. These people have passive aggressive behaviors and use these tendencies to always get their way or prevent you from doing or saying anything they don't like.

Perhaps you have been in this kind of a relationship before or you're still in one now and you don't have the slightest idea as the manipulation could be subtle and deceptive. The people who use these behaviors often leave their partners (or friends and family), confused. It can also be overt, demanding, and shaming that often leaves the other person immobilized.

Overt and Covert Emotional Manipulation

Overt emotional manipulation happens when one person resorts to intense and deliberate confrontation that will challenge the legitimacy or value of your issues. In extreme cases, it can be a form of bullying. In most cases, it's a matter of *posturing*. Some people become uncomfortable with assertion, and it doesn't take much of this type of posturing tactics for them to back down.

Covert manipulation on the other hand is subtler, and often people use a non-verbal gesture, a specific facial expression, a stare, or a shrug to get what they want. This form of deceitful behavior can be slightly harder to spot, however my aim for this book is to show you exactly how to do just that.

In any case, both forms of manipulation, overt and covert are more effective when the manipulator is good at communicating emoti0nal resolve, tenacity, and determination, thus sending a strong message to the other person that they are no match for their skills. When the other person is prone to self-doubt, they eventually get *defeated*.

So my plan in the succeeding chapters is to give you an overall account of general manipulative measures but more importantly an in-depth discussion about how to spot and defend against covert emotional manipulation as it's so crucial to eradicate from your life.

CHAPTER 2

HOW TO SPOT COVERT
MANIPULATION

Essentially where there are people there will be some degree of overt emotional manipulation, its unavoidable. However this is especially true when their is someone who wants to control or overpower you, who will resort to using *deceptive and underhanded tactics* for the sole purpose of altering your perceptions, behavior, and thinking.

Covert emotional manipulation usually occurs under the level of your conscious awareness. If you fall prey to this, you're often not even aware that you are being psychologically captive by the other person, which is why it's sometimes so difficult to spot.

Skilled emotional manipulators can easily make you doubt your sense of self-worth and emotional well-being, and in the process, letting them control you. The moment you succumb to this *trap*, the manipulator can easily strip you of your self-esteem and your identity, until nothing's left in you.

Experts refer to skilled manipulators as covert aggressive people. They often employ the following tactics in conjunction with one another usually without the target of their manipulation ever noticing:

- Hide their aggressive intentions.

- Make you afraid, doubt yourself, until you eventually give in or concede.

There are a few other tactics that they use regularly, which, are generally effective in manipulating unsuspecting individuals. It is important for people to recognize these tactics and learn how to respond to them to keep one from being sucked into their manipulator's bubble. *Self-empowerment is the key!*

"Dangerous" Manipulators

Highly skilled emotional manipulators can utilize just about any type of behavior to accomplish their hidden goals. They are even more dangerous when this person is good at "reading" behavioral patterns and actions of the target of their manipulation.

Let's call the *covert aggressor* as CA for now, and the object of their manipulation tactics is the *opponent*. When the CA knows their opponent inside and out (like their beliefs, insecurities, fears, weaknesses, level of conscientiousness, sensitivities, etc.), the CA can easily overpower them by using these behaviors against their opponent.

In extreme cases, experts suggest that manipulators may become full scale psychopaths, although I would argue that manipulation is just one facet of a whole host of psychological issues when it comes to these legitimately ill individuals. But in everyday life there are others who are just narcissists, and there are some that are *pick-up or con artists.*

Psychopaths consider themselves as the superior kind, who see others as prey. These people are not capable of giving love and empathy. They don't feel any remorse or guilt for whatever they do or may have done. For them, life is just a game of taking control and getting what they want, no matter how much it takes. It's unlikely you will come across anyone who truly has this condition as they are very few and far between and modern society is getting better all of the time at identifying them and giving them the help that they need.

However we are more concerned with the skilled covert manipulators you will come across in the office, at school or simply meet on the street. These types of people find it very difficult to have real relationships. They painstakingly take time to study people – their weaknesses, their strengths, their dreams, their desires, and most crucially their fears. They will not think twice to use these against you and a whole host of other manipulation tactics that they have mastered just to overpower you (if you allow them).

There is one factor you must always keep in mind. *Manipulators always want to be in control.* They are hungry for power and they won't stop until they achieve that goal, even if it means harming other people. If you're feeling less confident, less strong, less intelligent, less superior, or any other aspect of your life that you feel "less than" anything you were before, you may well be being manipulated.

Are you in a relationship right now? Do you remember when you first met the person? Was it something magical? *Manipulators are very often sweet-talkers.* They can easily hide their real plans and their real personalities – that's what they do, that's how highly skilled they can be. Their main goal is to trick you into believing that they care about you, and that they love you.

They will make you believe that they will do anything for you. They will get you hooked deeply, until you show your vulnerability, then manipulation and extreme abuse can follow (again if you let it). Soon, you will notice that what started out to be an ideal relationship, has become demeaning, exploitative, and confusing. You will notice that your self-esteem will slowly turn into doubt and you will eventually blame yourself for that.

When the manipulator gets full control, you will soon be amenable to *getting mere crumbs out of the interaction.* Soon, the person will not be concerned about discussing your emotions, needs, and fears. They don't care about them, anyway.

You will soon be blaming yourself for everything that's going wrong. You'll begin to over-analyze things, until you become so confused with what's really happening in your life. Every aspect of your day can suffer – your career, your social relationships, your mental well-being and even your physical health.

The next chapter will give you an idea of the types and qualities of people that make them vulnerable to manipulation so hopefully you can avoid many of these where possible.

CHAPTER 3

MANIPULATORS & THEIR TARGETS

"Controllers, abusers and manipulative people don't question themselves. They don't ask themselves if the problem is them. They always say the problem is someone else"

(Darlene Ouimet)

Before going into any depth on how to *fight back* manipulation tactics, it is necessary to discuss what makes people vulnerable to these *attacks* in the first place. How do skilled manipulators know that an individual can easily be manipulated? How do they choose their targets?

Understanding manipulation and manipulative behaviors will help you properly handle whatever situation you are in. Maybe you are living with a manipulative person, and you still don't know about it. As mentioned earlier, manipulators know how to go around your thoughts and your feelings, without you having the slightest hint that they are manipulating you (at first).

Manipulation exists in relationships, simply because it works! When manipulative people are presented with the opportunity to overpower others, they immediately grab it. The only way to fight back is to disable a manipulator's tactics, which we'll explore in greater detail later on.

But how do you do this in general? By learning more about and understanding how manipulation works, how manipulators do what they do, and the tactics they use. There are certain types of manipulative tactics that are easy to see, but there are some that are subtler that you cannot decipher what is happening, the covert type I mentioned previously.

Covert manipulators are usually much more skilled and calculative. So, when their tactics are exposed, rendering them ineffective, they will dig deeper into their arsenals and change their approach. If they are still ineffective, they will eventually leave you alone and find another victim. To say that when the people they are manipulating begin to fight back, they back off, and find other people they can control.

Most manipulators vehemently dislike having to work hard at manipulating people and thereby target the most vulnerable for the most part. They do the things they do because it comes out naturally for them but they still would prefer an easy ride. Hence, it is important for you to increase your understanding of their motives and their tactics, so you'll know if people are manipulating you or not.

Here are some of the most important things to know about manipulators and the the tactics they employ:

- Remember that manipulators will *never have a moment of insight and change overnight.* It's just not possible. These people are incapable of suddenly understanding what they have done to hurt. Hence, it's not effective to point out to a manipulator their shortcomings or how much they are hurting you. It's just not in them – they will never change just because you asked them to.

- No matter what you do, you will never be able to *out-manipulate* a highly skilled manipulator. When you begin to see that you are in a relationship with such a person, pay close attention to what they are doing, focus on how they are acting rather than what he/she is merely saying to you. There is a big difference between the two.

Even if you ask the manipulator *why*, you can never get a truthful answer, so why should you bother? Even if you let the person know that you don't like what they are doing and that they are giving you so much pain and suffering, he/she will often not care. Your partner might even use this to their advantage.

You cannot change a manipulator, but you can always change yourself.

The moment you stop cooperating, complying, or pleasing them, they will eventually stop. As I mentioned, they don't want to work hard for it, so eventually they will take off.

Truth is, manipulators do not always know about their tactics. However, the most dangerous manipulators are those who study what their moves will be and are intentional in the behavior they exhibit. These are the ones who are unlikely to change.

Manipulating and controlling others comes naturally to them. These actions do not create any kind of inner turmoil, dissonance or guilt that they may be hurting other people or violating their rights. *They just don't care!*

If the emotional manipulation is *ego-congruent,* there might be a slight motivation to change. These people will eventually use other tactics, but they will never change their beliefs. Their drive will always be the outcome, and not their own desire of becoming a better person.

There is another side of manipulation, wherein the manipulative individuals are not aware that they are being manipulative. When they are confronted, they are shocked and would feel bad about it. These are the people who still have a chance of changing their behaviors. I have many friends who showed glimpses of this type of behavior when we were growing up. But eventually every adult spots it within themselves and eradicates it with openness and honesty.

However truly manipulative individuals usually stay preoccupied with their own needs. They are not capable of feeling empathy towards the subject of their manipulative tactics. Even if they are made aware of how their target is hurting, they will not be motivated to change. *If their tactics become futile, they just go on and search for another victim.*

They will likely disguise their motives by hiding behind layers upon layers of lies. Skilled manipulators are aware that their erroneous behavior is unacceptable, hence, they will use tactics that are more socially acceptable:

- They will resort to loving and caring for their targets for a time. They will show their targets how deeply they care for them so the person will do the things they ask them to do. *"I am just doing this because I love you so much and I care for you..."*

- Manipulators will overpower you by making you feel that they are the experts. *"You should believe me when I tell you this because this is how it is supposed to be done. I should know, I studied this."*

- They will show you how generous they are. They will show you they care by helping you any way they can. *"Remember that I am doing this for your own good. I don't have anything to get out of this, you know."*

- They will make you feel that they need to do this for you. *"I am doing this because I have the obligation to do that, it's for your own good."*

It is futile to ask manipulators what their true motives and intentions are. You won't get any honest answer because they will become defensive and will manifest anger towards you. They will be in denial, this is the best defense mechanism that they know. Most manipulators even think they deserve to achieve their end goals, whatever it takes, because they feel that the universe owes them that.

What makes you vulnerable to manipulation?

Experts have identified certain habits, activities, scenarios, and behaviors that leave you open to manipulation. This doesn't mean that you may be doing something wrong which makes you vulnerable, these are just factors that *may* make you a *target* of skilled manipulators. These are general categories:

- *You are in transition.* You may be considering making changes in your life. You might be at the crossroads and still contemplating on what to do. This is a good entry point for manipulators as you are in what some psychotherapist's term "transition uncertainty." This might be changing jobs, moving house or just going through a breakup of some kind. You are often left open to manipulative strategies here as your thinking isn't as concrete as it typically might be.

- *You recently suffered a substantial loss.* Similar to going through a transition I mentioned above, you may also be experiencing financial issues with your business or have been laid off from your job or even the loss of a family member. During this time, if you are again unsure of exactly what you should be doing. Then a manipulator may pretend to be coming to rescue you, but in truth, you have just become an easy prey.

- *You may be experiencing a time of instability and uncertainty.* Things may not be going right in every aspect of your life right now, and you're looking for people to turn to. While you have friends and family, you may still get easily distracted when a manipulator shows interest in you. It is easier to influence people who are not in the *"right state of mind"* as they are often looking for some form of support and guidance which may be coming from someone without the persons best interests at heart.

- *You entertain negative thoughts and emotions, like fear, anxiety, and uncertainty to frequently.* I write about this more extensively within "Emotional Intelligence: A Psychologists Guide" but you could be worrying excessively about how things are going to turn out. Or you tend to be anxious about work, family, and life in general, that you fail to see all the good things. Manipulators see this negativity as an easy way in to influence your thinking further.

- *You get easily discouraged, upset, or depressed.* When things don't go your way, you tend to be discouraged immediately. You easily get upset when another person does something that you do not approve of, or may have caused you harm. Or you get easily depressed in the face of challenging situations.

This is an opening some manipulators wait for because these emotions can throw a person out of balance. You are easily controlled because you are confused and your mind is in disarray. A skilled manipulator would come to you to make you feel that you are not alone and when they gain your trust, that's when they take advantage.

- *You easily believe what people tell you.* Some people are too gullible to a fault. This makes you vulnerable because skilled manipulators are good talkers. They can simply sweet talk their way into your heart and into your life. Then you'll never know that they are beginning to control everything about you.

- *You easily become too blinded by love.* Manipulators will make you fall hard for them. They will do everything to make you believe that they love you. Even when issues arise, you'd still be too blind-sided to see the signs. Loving someone too much makes you believe that the other person will never hurt you.

  They would often tell you, *"if you love me, you will do this for me"*. Because you do, you will follow blindly. You'll stop questioning them and the things that they want you to do. You will be smitten and you'll never even know what hit you.

- *You get easily attached to people and things.* Similar to falling in love too easily, when you get easily attached to other people and situations in general, it's easier to manipulate you. Have you become clingy? Manipulators can take advantage.

- *You constantly look for approval.* A skilled manipulator will take advantage of this. Initially, they will make you feel that they are your knight in shining armor. They will let you feel that they appreciate you, that they see the real you, and they like you for you. They will satisfy this need and when you're too attached to them, that is when the behavior usually starts to change.

- *You constantly seek help in every decision you make.* If you are always relying on other people to decide things for you. If it is hard for you to make decisions because you don't want to be making the wrong ones. A manipulator will seize this opportunity.

- *You are perceived as "too nice".* If you are always "too nice" to everyone, it is easy for manipulators to befriend you, and eventually, control much more about you than you would like. This may happen because you just can't say *no* to someone that you care about, especially when they have shown you how good they were. You may be naïve to the fact you can't see what is behind the façade of the other person.

- *You can be too trusting.* Along the same lines as being too nice, people who will just trust anyone who says that they only have their well-being in mind, can also be easily manipulated.

Can you recognize the hooks?

So having looked at some of the overarching personality traits which might make a person susceptible to manipulative behavior, it's also wise to be able to spot some of the triggers. Expert manipulators will target the areas of your personality which can help them get what they want.

At this point, think about what you want to achieve in your life. What do you fear losing the most? When you don't know what you want, manipulators can use that to show you what you might want and desire. And because you are easily manipulated, you'll agree with whatever the other person will be telling you.

When you know exactly what your desires are, it will be harder for a manipulator to talk you into wanting otherwise. Knowing yourself makes you a difficult target, even for skilled manipulators.

Do you have a strong desire to find love and security? Or is money or career your top priority? Do you look for sexual fulfillment or attention from someone you care about? Are you afraid of getting old? Or dying alone or unhappy? Are you afraid of losing your job or everything that you have?

When you are aware of your fears and desires, you will also be aware that manipulators can use these to control you. It is easy to spot a manipulator if you know what to look for, the personality traits and hooks they are weeding out. *(This will be discussed in detail in the succeeding chapters.)*

CHAPTER 4

WHY DO PEOPLE DO THE THINGS THEY DO?

Why did he do that? What were his intentions?

What led her to behave in that way?

Why is she so stubborn?

Why doesn't he listen to me?

We are all amateur psychologists to some extent. We all pass judgment to others, often unnecessarily. We are all guilty of shifting blame. When something bad happens, people try to make sense of it any way they can, and sometimes find someone else to pin the mistake on. Wouldn't life be easier if we knew the reason behind a certain behavior, action, or thought?

Every person has their own perception of things – what you believe is wrong, could be right for another. It's just how humans are. It's just how the mind works. But sometimes, when you become totally frustrated with a person who doesn't seem to understand what you want from them, or when you cannot understand why your spouse is acting differently lately, you'd want to know why exactly people do the things we do.

People have their own minds. We are all different. There is no two persons alike, even twins for that matter. It's a fact that people are different, and the real question is why! Is may be due to their gender, or culture, their nationality, or maybe their environment, or someone is just plain and simply difficult? Or is there a deeper reason to why people are different?

Is it because of emotions? How about thoughts? Feelings, habits, or impulses? Whilst on the surface it may appear that there are these individual and cultural differences, however when you dig a little deeper you find that we are all more similar than you may think.

Different Motivations

There is an unwritten rule in actions and behaviors, and that is people act based on what motivates them. People act and do things differently because of the difference in their needs and wants, and the variety of strategies that can be attempted to attain them.

There is no right or wrong answer here, because people have a concept of what's right for them, it's just a matter of perception. People, however, share the same core needs in reality which means that why personalities might change on the surface, essentially everyone is the same boat in this sense. *Maslow's Pyramid or "hierarchy of needs" clearly shows us this.*

For instance, more than one human need motivates you, hence, there is also a variety of reasons for each of our actions. We may have similar core needs, but we have varying degrees of awareness when it comes to the relationship between our needs and our actions and behaviors.

When you are not aware of what you need, you end up acting and behaving based on your thoughts, impulse, habits, and feelings. Each of these motivation types can be a reason to take responsibility for the choices we may make. Everything that we do is connected to our needs, until we do things that will specifically get us any underlying needs that we have, then we will continue to act without thinking about how we can achieve things beyond our needs.

Thoughts and Feelings

People often do things because they felt they had to do it. Most of the time, happiness, joy, and satisfaction will lead you to do things that will give you such feelings. On the other hand, fear, guilt, and shame, may lead you to avoid certain things.

Feelings are immediately translated into actions, sometimes, without understanding what you truly want. Most of the time, the feelings tend to give a more commanding action, so that, you don't have the opportunity to think and understand your feelings first.

I describe the influence of our primitive limbic system and the effects it exhibits over our emotional state at length in other books, but I will copy a passage here below to describe more clearly what I mean. It's from a chapter within Emotional Intelligence called "Living Our Limbic Legacy":

The Old Mammalian Brain

"However what isn't in doubt is the development and influence of the limbic system on our psychological behaviors when it comes to emotional intelligence influences brought about by human interaction. Basically any thought that originates in the spinal cord must pass through the "rational" part of the brain, the frontal cortexes in order to be rationalized, conceptualized and understood.

However before it reaches these structures a thought must pass through the limbic system, the more primitive part of the brain where they become "emotionally charged" meaning that we have an emotional reaction to an event before the complex cognitive prefrontal lobe can engage and make sense of it.

"The emotional brain responds to an event more
quickly than the thinking brain"

(Daniel Goleman)

The limbic system isn't a single structure within the brain but rather a set of structures which are located on both sides of the thalamus and positioned just below the cerebrum. It is sometimes referred to as the paleomammalian cortex or the "old mammalian brain" owing to the time period in which it evolved within us.

Essentially these were the first structures that set us apart from our reptilian ancestors, an addition and upgrade of hardware to the primitive structures of the archipallium which is comprised of the brain stem, medulla, cerebellum and oldest basal nuclei. These structures are primarily concerned with just the base sensory organs and simple motor functions, the starting point of any complex organism.

But the limbic system can do much more than this, as a system it supports a host of other functions including emotional regulation, long-term memory capability, ambition and all types of motivational behavior in general. It is basically the driving seat of our emotion center, as the structures heavily influence the endocrine system which intern regulates the dopermaneric pleasure responses to natural and recreational 'highs' alike.

The limbic system also has heavy input on the autonomic nervous system which mediates the 'fight or flight' response within us which can have many knock-on effects to our emotional state as well. However all of these elements are still very base and primitive components with regards to the human biological make-up but which still affect our day-to-day lives in a big way even today.

As much as we try to escape this ancestral legacy with the development of the outer neocortexes which provides the machinery that primes us for complex decision making cognition, we are constantly held back by an undersized prefrontal lobe and over powering limbic system. Don't get me wrong, I would certainly rather live in a world that allowed for the emotions of love, connection and compassion which the limbic system affords, but the flip side of this is fear, jealously and aggression which is elicited from these primal centers in exactly the same way.

Now you might be wondering what exactly this has to do with emotional intelligence and the answer is in a monumental way. Essentially what you are doing when you are attempting to develop E.I. is foster the positive parts of this limbic system activity i.e. bonding, rapport building and compassion whilst downplaying the negative side such as fear, anxiety and anger.

Emotional intelligence also comes heavily into play when trying to read someone to develop the social awareness aspects of E.I. which are crucial. What you are actually attempting to do is read the emotional cues the other person is giving away. The physiological changes the body produces naturally, unconsciously and automatically which is almost impossible to mask. This may include getting flush in the face when embarrassed or perspiring when nervous. Trying to control the volume and tonality of the voice when angry or fidgety movements of the body when anxious, it's very difficult to do.

These physiological responses were once highly useful as they were the only means for us to communicate what we were thinking or feeling. They are still very relevant even in today's world of modern speech with regards to conveying emotion, and this can certainly work in your favor when developing the social E.I. you are looking for.

Essentially emotional intelligence requires very effective symbiosis and communication between the newer wet wear of the rational brain with older more primitive emotional structures of the limbic system. There is a term for this communicative ability and brain development in general which neuroscientists refer to a "neuroplasticity". It's basically the process of forming new neural pathways and connections in the brain in response to new learning.

Using certain strategies to develop your own E.Q. levels is no different. When performing these learning techniques you are strengthening the billions of microscopic neuron pathways lining the road between the old emotional centers and the newer rational structures. This also allows for these pathways to branch out, much like a tree to form new connections with surrounding cells again improving overall capacity and cognitive ability. It has been estimated that a single cell can grow up to 15,000 new connections with its surrounding neighbors.

This process essentially further increases the rate of the positive feedback loops and ensures that like anything else which is practiced consistently and over time, it becomes habitual in nature and easier to perform in the future. Emotional intelligence is therefore a skill which is learned like any other"

So as you can see there is clear separation between the "Thinker and "Feeler" within every person and they can often pull in very different directions. This is what ultimately leaves some people open to manipulative behavior, if the above two are not congruently aligned.

Your feelings compel you to do things from within, while your thoughts will compel you to do things from without. This is an important distinction to make because the freedom of being able to choose rather than being compelled to do things is a huge difference.

Making a choice is always internal – it's always up to the individual if he/ she will do something or not. Most people take into consideration the consequences of their actions and what others will think of them, before making a choice or a decision. There is a difference between believing that you need to do something, and in choosing things based on what's truly important.

So, your thoughts contain a variety of information about the things that are important to you, and in that way, the expressions of your needs. Some people may lack the vibrancy of feelings – like the sense of simply being alive. It doesn't matter if you are living it happily or not, what's important is that you are handling the experience well.

People who manage their feelings well, simple have more control.

CHAPTER 5

WARNING SIGNS THAT YOU ARE BEING MANIPULATED

"The truth will set you free, but first it will make you miserable"

(James Garfield)

Sometimes you have to concede that emotional manipulation is difficult to detect, simply because skilled manipulators can be subtle. They are like undercover agents, being able to control you for a while before you can figure out what is happening, exactly. *That is, if ever you do figure it out! Manipulators are like puppet masters!*

You could easily become an unsuspecting puppet if you fail to notice the signs of manipulation. Like puppets, when your strings are pulled in the direction that your manipulator decides on, you may find yourself following without question.

Psychologists are convinced that a victim of emotional manipulation could probably know that *something is going wrong,* however, they cannot recognize what exactly is the matter. You may have been manipulated before, or you're still in a manipulative relationship, but you don't exactly know for sure.

The truth is, ***knowing that someone you care about is manipulating you is easier than you might think it is.***

You may be able to learn and even memorize covert manipulation techniques, but you don't need to know much about the techniques they use, just to know that you are feeling something different. *Don't look at their actions, rather look at yourself. Look at your feelings if you feel you are being manipulated, your emotions wont lie to you.*

Manipulative people can be anyone – your spouse, your boyfriend/girlfriend, your close friend, or even a new acquaintance. In any relationship that you have, there could be someone who has been trying to control you.

These are the signs to watch out for:

- **Will bring you to home court.**

    A skilled manipulator will insist on meeting you in a physical space where they can get the upper hand and take control. It could be at their home, office, or even their car. It can be any place where they feel familiarity and ownership (wherein, you don't have).

- **Allowing you to speak first to look for your weaknesses.**

Salespeople often use this tactic in a more "feeling out" fashion. A skilled salesman will ask you general and probing questions first. This will enable them to establish a baseline to give them an idea of your behavior and the way you think. They will use their findings to determine your strengths and your weaknesses.

This is a similar form of questioning that manipulative people use in order to conceal a hidden agenda. This can occur in your work place or even within your personal relationships.

- **Manipulating the facts.**

A skilled manipulator knows how to manipulate the facts. They are good at lying and making excuses, so that they become the victim, and you become their offender. There will be exaggerations in their story. They may even resort to withholding valuable information. They will create a situation that will picture you as someone who can't be trusted.

- **Resorting to intellectual bullying.**

There are people who resort to intellectual bullying. They are the know-it-all individuals who will take advantage of you by imposing alleged statistics and facts that you may have little knowledge of. This may occur in negotiations, discussions, financial/sales situations as well as in your personal arguments.

By making you feel that they are the expert, the manipulator will sway you through their agenda without you even realizing what is happening. Some manipulators use this technique because they want to have that sense of *intellectual superiority*.

- **Exposing your weaknesses and target you when you least expect it.**

The moment you let a manipulative individual know your weaknesses, they can easily use them to control you. They will highlight your weaknesses and show you that they can be your strength. This will be the beginning of them, controlling you. They will make you feel that you need them, but truth is you don't.

They will make humiliating comments about your appearance, belittle your credentials and background, or emphasize your old model smart phone. They will also flag you for running late for an important meeting or how bad your last project went. They are good at making you look bad and incapable. They will make sure that you feel their *psychological superiority* over you.

They'll appear as if they are concerned though. They will offer to help you overcome your weaknesses, but little do you realize that they are using these weaknesses to have a hold on you.

- **Overwhelming you with raised tone of voice.**

One rather obvious way to know if you are being manipulated is when your significant other consistently raises their voice during disagreements, or even during simple discussions. This type is called *aggressive manipulation*. They use their voice loud enough so that you will give them what they want. Often, they will use strong body language while they speak loudly, this include exaggerated hand gestures or standing upright.

- **Resorting to negative surprises.**

Skilled manipulators also use negative surprises to distract you, while they work on gaining psychological advantage over you. What should raise a red flag is the manner in which the negative information is revealed, it's usually presented without warning. Thus, you are given little time to think and prepare a plan to counter their actions.

- **Leaving you no time to decide.**

Running along the same lines as the above, when you are in a discussion with an individual and you take time to decide on something, the manipulator will step it up and put pressure on you until you decide, albeit hastily. They may use concerns about time being important. They will apply tension to control you, in the hopes that you will crack and just give in to them. You are not given the opportunity to think before you make decision.

- **Resorting to criticisms and judgmental words.**

Often, manipulators do not mince their words, they make unnecessary critical remarks that they may disguise what they are saying as a playfulness or sarcasm. You will then feel inferior, helpless, and less secure. They will look at anything trivial and make comments about these things. For example, the manipulator may constantly comment about a whole host of things, how bad you look in your dress, or how old your smart phone is etc. They will attempt to make you look bad and unworthy.

- **Overwhelming you with procedures, paperwork, and red tape.**

Another method manipulators use to take control is through unnecessary bureaucracy. They will present you with many people to deal with, procedures to get through, laws to consider, and other roadblocks that will throw you off guard. This will make things more difficult for you but they *will be there to help you*. They will resort to this so that you won't look at the facts, seek for truth, hide flaws, and even evade being probed.

- **Giving you the silent treatment.**

Skilled manipulators will deliberately not answer your calls, emails, text messages, and other inquiries. They will overpower you by making you wait and make you doubt things. They use the silent treatment as leverage. They resort to mind games to throw you off track and instil uncertainty in your mind.

- **Resorting to playing dumb.**

Some will even resort to pretending to be ignorant. They will make it appear that they don't understand what you want, or what you want them to do. They will make you take on the responsibility and let you work hard for it. Manipulators use this technique to avoid obligations and responsibilities.

- **Eliciting guilt-baiting.**

Manipulators can target your soft spot and resort to *unreasonable blaming*. They will hold you responsible for their happiness or unhappiness. By doing so, they can easily coerce you into giving in to unreasonable demands and requests.

- **Playing victim.**

  Some will resort to telling exaggerated personal and health issues, most of which are indeed imagined. They will try to get your sympathy by deliberately showing you how frail they are and how much they need you. They will play weak and exploit your good will. They will shrug at your guilty conscience and your sense of obligation. They will tap into your nurturing instinct for them to get you to do things for them.

- **Resorting to emotional blackmail.**

  Following on from the previous two points, if you are in a relationship and someone tells you that they will kill themselves if you leave them, then you are in a manipulative relationship. It's their form of intimidation and guilt-tripping. Some would even resort to rage, like when they point out that they couldn't believe that you can hurt them.

- **Implementing the foot-in-door strategy.**

  Your spouse might ask something small and easy of you and after you agree to it, they will immediately make a follow-up with the *real request*. You will now be put in a tight spot where it would be difficult for you to say no. Because if you do say no, they will be upset/hurt and make you feel like you're the bad one in the relationship. When you begin to justify and defend yourself, they'll know that they got the upper hand and it will just be a matter of time before you can say yes to the *real request*.

- **Resorting to humor and joking around.**

  A manipulative partner always makes you feel intimidated and embarrassed whenever you're with them or out with your other friends. When your friend tries to confront your partner for insulting you, your manipulative partner will immediately declare that everything was just a joke, and that they were just kidding around. However, the other people who *actually listened* will know the real meaning behind that *joke*.

It is important to be aware of these different tactics and watch out for them when you can, and soon you'll be able to decipher them at will. This however is not an exhaustive list, but for the meantime, the techniques above are the most commonly used, so this list will be a helpful place to start.

PART 2

TECHNIQUES AND PRACTICAL STRATEGIES TO COMBAT MANIPULATION IT IN THE REAL WORLD

Avoiding being manipulated can be easier said then done, but if you're armed with the right tools, you have a much better chance to detect it when it does happen and from a safer distance. It's just about having the right and effective strategies to counter this type of behavior.

For this part of the book, we will look at the art of verbal and non-verbal communication. I will also be giving you tips on how to be a master of persuasion and influence. You will also be given practical tips on how to deal with a manipulative person and if you're in a relationship with them, how you can get out yourself out of it. You will also be given tips on how to raise your overall self-esteem which makes the biggest impact in terms of avoiding manipulative behavior.

CHAPTER 6

MASTERING THE MECHANICS OF VERBAL AND NON-VERBAL COMMUNICATION

"The basic tool for the manipulation of reality is the manipulation of words. If you can control the meaning of words, you can control the people who must use the words"

(Philip Dick)

People are constantly communicating with one another, for every minute of every day. Whether this is with the words they are speaking or the body language they are exhibiting, you will always be portraying something to someone. Manipulators can just be considered to have above average skills in this department, otherwise, how can they be so good at what they do?

There are two aspects of communication in general, *verbal and non-verbal*. This chapter will explain to you the difference between the two and give you some techniques on how to efficiently use them in dealing with the people around you.

The Importance of Communication

The truth is, the human species are pack of animals. Our ancestors lived as hunters and they gathered as a group, and they depended on one another for companionship, sustenance and protection where communication was key.

What differentiates us from other animals is that we have developed the outer cortex's of our brains to the point that we can communicate in much more than a primitive sense. We have developed the complex structures of the larynx like the vocal cords enabling us to interact both verbally and non-verbally. Again the impact of the limbic system on this process can't be overstated.

Communication shapes out relationships and interactions with other people in every way possible. When we are able to understand the different aspects of verbal and non-verbal communication and the importance this has on our daily interactions, we are already a step further in enhancing positive relationships.

What is Verbal Communication?

Verbal communication is anything that involves words, whether spoken, written, or signaled (sign language). The conversation you had this morning with your son, or the news you were reading online, even the text message you sent to your spouse asking if they can pick you up after work, is a form of verbal communication.

Your ability to communicate a specific language depends on an *organized system of words*, rather than mere sounds, which is what sets humans apart from the other primate species. Technology has even allowed humans to speak with one another even when there is physical distance.

Why Verbal Communication is Important

Verbal communication is an integral part of our lives because we use it to express ourselves and the thoughts/feelings we have in more articulate ways. We use it to inform people, whether of our needs or to share what we know.

Clarification is one of the most important components of verbal communication. There are individuals who are more articulate, while there are some who have difficulty expressing their thoughts in spoken words. If people do not speak with one another, there will always be misunderstandings and actions will constantly be misconstrued.

Verbal communication is obviously an excellent tool in using the power of persuasion.

What is Non-Verbal Communication?

Non-verbal communication on the other hand includes your body language - everything from facial expressions, gestures, posture, and eye contact. The sound of your voice is a big component of non-verbal communication, and it includes your tone, pitch, and volume.

There are instances when the meaning behind a person's words is entirely different than the literal translation, examples are mockery and sarcasm. Your clothing choice is also a part of what you are communicating to others without speaking, which is often the basis of people's opinion of you.

When you want to know what the real intentions of a person are, you should always look for the things that they are not saying, because body language does not lie.

It's a fairly well agreed upon fact that non-verbal communication makes up for a large part of what a person is saying and how it is being interrupted. Albert Mehrabian is a professor of psychology at ULCA and his communication research theory points this out. His studies primarily focused on interactions with heavy emotional and 'feeling' elements to them as opposed to normal everyday situations so are especially relevant for a discussion on emotional manipulation.

Mehrabian is considered somewhat of a grandfather of modern body language study and non-verbal communication theory due to his work on the subject through the mid to late 1900's. The figures that people most often quote from him come from two papers he published in 1967 which found that around:

- 7% of the message pertaining to the feelings and emotions of an interaction comes from the actual word(s) which are spoken.

- 38% comes from the paralinguistic element i.e. the way in which the words are said.

- 55% coming from the facial expressions.

So it's easy to see how important these non-verbal and gesture elements play in regards to overall communication, especially in an emotional sense. However this concept is also beneficial to keep in mind during phone conversations where you will not be able to showcase your gestures. You will have only your voice to converse with the other person and this will require some level of modulation through the course of the conversation.

Mastering the Art of Communication

This section will briefly discuss how you can up your game in terms of your communication skills. How you can use these skills to increase your discernment for other people's intentions. It helps in every possible way to be a good communicator, so that people won't take advantage of any weaknesses they might discover while talking with you.

There are a lot of tools available to you in your interactions with other people. You just need to be learn how to use them accordingly.

Verbal Communication

#1 Words/Vocabulary

Your vocabulary and the actual words you choose to speak are obviously the most important tools when it comes to verbal communication, hence, you need to choose what you say wisely. Words are powerful, they have the ability to put one person into a position of strength whilst simultaneously bringing another down.

If a person is using rudimentary vocabulary then ensure that you make use of simple language yourself that is free from ambiguity. If however they are using a greater range of diction, then attempt to adjust yours to match it accordingly.

Having a wide lexicon enhances your communication skills and draws people into you. An experienced manipulator will often take advantage of this. Don't get yourself caught in a web of lies of a skilled manipulator, just because you have a limited vocabulary.

#2 Tone and Pace

Your vast vocabulary or your mastery of words are of little consequence if other people cannot understand them. The pace with which you speak can say a lot. Talking too fast may mean you are excited about something. On the other hand, speaking at a slower pace may mean you want the other person to understand what you're saying.

The volume of your voice is also an important factor. You can draw your audience to listen to you with clear and loud voice. However, proper voice projection is necessary, especially in personal interactions, where you need to shift your volume accordingly.

#3 Enunciation

Enunciation is an integral part of the communication process. Clear enunciation would often give you an edge. It is important that you clearly enunciate your words to avoid misinterpretation and miscommunication.

Non-Verbal Communication

#1 Hands

Hand gestures are a form of non-verbal communication. You can tell a lot about people by observing their hand-positioning. People use hand movements when trying to prove a point or emphasize an idea.

Overall the arms and hands are a defensive barrier to the body and indicate openness and security when in a neutral position by a person's side and conversely apprehension and insecurity when crossed in front of the chest. In fact holding anything in front of the body like a bag or papers for instance will signify this barrier being built.

It is estimated that the hands contain more neural connections to the brain than any other peripheral body part and for good reason, we use the hands to navigate almost everything in the physical world by touch and can both consciously and unconsciously signal such a wide range of intentions as a result. They are able to give standalone signals with regards to the direction they are pointing or in conjunction with other body parts in the form of holding, clenching, scratching and tapping just to illustrate a few.

Hands are involved in everything from handshakes when greeting to waving for goodbyes. Along with the fingers they can make the more obvious expressive signals like the western style 'thumbs up' or 'OK' sign to indicate contentment or validity of a point which is being made.

#4 Eyes

Eyes are what we predominantly use to assess the world around us, but it works both ways. Not only do we use them to look out at the world, it has long been stated that looking into the eyes of another can tell you a great deal about their internal thoughts and feelings.

"The eyes are the windows to the soul"

(William Shakespeare)

Eyes are simply mesmerizing by their very nature and play a large role when it comes to hypnosis techniques. Even making strong eye contact with a stranger on the street can feel like a significant event. However with regards to manipulation we are actually more concerned with eye movement more than anything. To say the direction in which the gaze changes in relation to the behavior of others and questioning.

The following observations are intended to help you with just that, to give you any idea of what people are really thinking regarding their eye movement. For the sake of these descriptions 'left' and 'right' side are in relation to the individual and not the observer.

So in general a person will predominantly look to one side when being asked a question. They will either look left or right when reflecting, recalling or remembering information. The side in which they look relates to the side of the brain they are accessing by and large. The right hand side being more concerned with creativity, emotions and feeling whilst the left hand side dealing with the facts, figures and memory.

Now this is broadly speaking of course and there are other intricacies and nuances we will explore below. But in a general sense, assessing eye gaze/direction can be a very accurate indicator into someone's true thoughts/feelings and if they are attempting to be manipulative.

Overall if someone is looking to the right it means that they are creating something in their mind, they are tapping into the creative centers of the brain in an attempt to fabricate, guess and story tell. This obviously isn't an issue if you are asking them a question and they respond by looking right and saying something like "I'm not really sure, but I imagine it would be like this". They are genuinely being honest here by giving you an impression of how they think it would be and not stating they know it for sure.

However if they look right and say something like "I was in that situation last week and this is how it happened". This is more worrying as they are stating something as an affirmative, something they know to be true from a past experience and memory, however when responding they were accessing the creative/story telling part of the brain whilst they did it. This is not to say they are definitely lying but is a red flag none the less.

To really assess this better you need to pay attention to whether the person is also looking 'up' or 'down' whilst also looking to one side. In relation to the above example, if the person is looking downwards and to the right, this would indicate that they are accessing the creative areas of the brain but more in relation to emotion. They may just be recounting the feelings they had regarding the situation they are being asked about as opposed to actually fabricating the answer.

However if they are looking upwards whilst also looking right, this is more sinister as this would indicate that they are fully accessing the imagination centers of the brain and heavily suggests that they are indeed fabricating whatever response they are making.

Conversely looking left when answering such a question would signify they were genuinely accessing memory centers and are telling the truth. This is especially true if the person is looking upwards and to the left which indicates recollection from the memory and image centers of the brain greatly implying truthfulness in what they are saying.

Similarly looking downwards and to the left also indicates honesty as it's a cue for recounting self-talk and rationalization about a given situation or subject.

#5 Position / Posture

Confident speakers and communicators stand up straight and command authority. They don't slouch. They speak with authority. If you can do that, manipulative people will not see you as target and they will not bother you as much.

The importance of cultivating overall high levels of confidence in relation to achieving anything in life cannot be overstated and it will greatly feed into your emotional state. It's a little bit of a "chicken and egg" scenario in terms of confidence; you require at least some level of self-assurance before attempting anything. But you don't really reap the full rewards until you have completed the task, had the experience and gained confidence from it.

Needless to say, you can only develop a high level of confidence when you do eventually have full trust in yourself. So practice conversing from a position of strength. When you can communicate well, other people will not look at you as inferior.

When you can play with your words, speak with authority, and can easily discern hidden intentions by simply observing a person's non-verbal gestures, nobody can take advantage of you and manipulate you. So, make sure that you improve on all of your communication skills, both verbal and non-verbal.

CHAPTER 7

PRACTICAL INFLUENCE & PERSUASION SKILL SET

As most of us already know, the human mind can be easy to influence but it takes a certain knack to persuade others in the right way in order to get them to listen to you. Or conversely spot the influence tactics of manipulators in order to counteract them.

My academic life required me to extensively study people's minds from the inside in order to see what they might do on the outside. You will find that you will naturally be doing many of these things already, especially if you are a more empathetic and social person. But it's still a good idea to pin point exactly what you are doing right, why that it's working and to learn new skills that will push you to improve even further.

Human behavior is pretty much the most predictable thing on the planet. If you know these patterns on a personal level and on a wider societal level, then you can start play the game of influence and persuasion with a great deal of success.

Firstly I think it's a good idea to state exactly what persuasion is. It's simply the process or action taken by a person or group of people when they cause something to change. This will be in relation to another human being and something that changes their inner mental systems (attitudes, values & beliefs) or their external behavior patterns (actions & habits).

The act of persuasion may also create something new within the person or may just modify something that already exists in their mind. In terms of the process, persuasion is usually comprised of three parts:

1. The communicator or source of persuasion

2. The actual persuasive nature of the appeal

3. The target person/audience of the appeal

All three elements need to be taken into account before attempting any form of persuasion yourself. It's good practice to look around you in your daily life and watch out for when these subtle (and sometimes overt) persuasions are happening. It's good training for when you want to employ similar tactics yourself or just as importantly to make sure you are not on the end of something you do not want to be.

Experts say that people with good leadership quality and persuasion power utilize 10 influence techniques by and large:

- *Logical persuasion*

- *Legitimizing*

- *Stating*

- *Exchanging*

- *Appealing to relationship*

- *Socializing*

- *Consulting*

- *Alliance building*

- *Modeling*

- *Appealing to value*

The flip side of these are the four negative tactics people use: *threatening, intimidating, avoiding, and manipulating.* However these tactics are much easier to spot and are not employed by the most skillful manipulators for just that reason. Instead they have sharpened their skills in the more everyday persuasion methods in order to go under the radar with their actual intentions.

Manipulative individuals have greatly enhanced their communication skills in this sense. They can simply talk and influence others to follow their advice or do the things they want the other person to do. It is helpful to know about how the skills manipulative people use to effectively influence others to follow them or persuade others to do things for them.

So, *manipulating is just another form of persuading*, it's just an act of coercion by subtly pushing another person to do things against their best interests.

Persuasion and influence skills can certainly be learnt like any other technique in life. Part of the process of knowing if you are being manipulated and being able to overcome it, is to learn more about what people do to influence and persuade others to do things that they don't normally do.

There is a better way to make others do what you want.

The key is in getting other people to *buy into your idea, and end up wanting to do it your way by way of their own choice*. People have minds of their own, they are not stupid. You can't force them to do things for you without them truly being on board. To persuade people, you have to get others *to want what you want, but think that it was them who came to that decision.*

Now whilst I have had plenty of experience using persuasion in real life business and family situations, there are others who have academically studied the principles in greater depth. One of those is professor of psychology, Robert Cialdini.

According to Cialdini there are 6 major principles or "weapons" of persuasion. They are written with a more commercial context in mind, for selling and the advertising industry. But they can equally be applied to the psychology of human behavior on an interpersonal level.

I must say that I agree that they all play a part in successful persuasion at one time or another and they definitely serve as a good basis to explore and avoid manipulation as you will have a better understanding of the tactics they will use. So here is my overview of the techniques for you.

Cialdini's 6 "Weapons" of Influence

Reciprocity

The first principle of persuasion is reciprocity. It is based on the theory that when you offer something to someone, they will feel indebted and have an urge to reciprocate it back. Humans seem innately wired to feel this way and act like this from an evolutionary stand point; it appears that compassion for another person, especially when they have performed a kind act in your favor is hard not to reciprocate.

Counter to the "all for themselves" mentality painted by many historians (and some of the manipulators we see today) early human civilization had to be predicated largely on cooperation and community to survive and thrive. But this principle is still applicable to almost every situation in life today.

It can sometimes seem to be the most manipulative principle if you look at it in the wrong way. It is more advisable to cultivate a giving attitude in general and let this law play out naturally when employing it yourself. But manipulative people will engage it in the opposite way. Here are some things to do in order to use it to your advantage or to watch out for if you believe it's being used against you:

- A person will always make the first move. They offer something first in order to make the other person feel indebted to them.

- Next, they offer something they can only get from them where possible. If they give you something exclusive then it will further work in their favor.

- Personalize what is given so that it's known who it came from. Make it special for them so that they internalize the event more effectively.

Following these simple steps will help you persuade a person in some future interaction down the line. If you do these things enough and in the right way you shouldn't actually have to do much persuading at all, as the person will naturally jump at the chance to help you out to return the favor.

There have been experiments conducted in American restaurants where it was found that the more attention and generosity the waiter showcased, the higher he was tipped by customers. They would give the customers a toffee and receive an 18% tip. When they increased it to 2 toffees, they received a 21% tip in return. So the moral of the story is give out a lot of toffees, you never know what might come back.

Commitment & Consistency

It is human nature to settle for whatever has already been tried and tested in the mind. People will have a mental image of who they are and how things should be. I always think back to the analogy within the movie "The Matrix" when describing this principle to people where Laurence Fishburne's character Morpheus is explaining to Neo the concept of his 'residual self image', that his perception of himself within the matrix is merely a projection, a digital image of his mental self. This is true for people in everyday life too; they really want to remain consistent with what their values and beliefs align with and who they think they really are.

Most people will not be up for experimenting and act in a way they have always done so in the past. So to influence someone through this principle, you have to first get them to commit to something. It might seem a little tough to do so at first, as it requires a certain commitment on your part too, but following a few simple rules can help you with it. The following steps will help you in persuading a person through the consistency and commitment principle.

- Get the person to start small so that they can manage the change before they integrate it with their personality and get hooked on the habit.

- Get them to accept something publicly so they will feel the urge to stick with it and obligated to see it through.

- Reward the person for sticking to the course. Giving away rewards can help with strengthening a person's interest in whatever you are trying to get them to go along with.

Social Proof

This principle is another human tendency and one in which we tend to place a high amount of stock and trust in other people and their opinions on things we haven't tried for ourselves yet. This is especially relevant if the opinion is coming from a perceived/ credible expert or a close friend. Nobody has the time to try everything in life so we naturally have to rely on others and take cues from them on experiences we haven't yet had.

I'm sure you are drawn to products and services that are endorsed by experts just because you think they know what they are saying or equate a person's fame and celebrity with validity for the product, which is a very common marketing tactic every big company employs. The same extends to other people who will take to something if another trustworthy person endorses it.

Humans are pattern seekers by nature and we are continually looking to connect the dots of evidence around us and take shortcuts to the answers. Here is a closer look at some of the aspects of this theory.

- The first step will be to obtain credible support from experts in the field. This will work like a charm, as people will take to it instantly.

- As I mentioned above, most people like it if their favorite celebrity endorses a product. They will take a liking to it especially if the celebrity claims to use the product himself or herself.

- People prefer it if others like them are also indulging in the similar behavior. They will take to it if they find that someone else likes them doing it.

- Apart from individuals, people are also more comfortable when larger parts of the population approve of their behavior. A person is more likely to buy or do something if their friends and family members approve of it; people just love following the crowd as it makes them feel safe and accepted.

In a study conducted in 1935, many subjects were placed in a dark room with a small dot of light in the distance. The subjects were asked to observe the dot and guess how many times it moved. Each of the participants had a different answer they gave when initially asked.

However when all of them were assembled in one room and had time to discuss the outcome and then asked the same question they all agreed on just one unanimous answer that was in fact much different from what they had originally guessed. These types of studies have been conducted for over a hundred years and even before Cialdini wrote about them within the 1980's.

Today the internet is awash with social proof examples especially when it comes to social media and online advertising. Companies are desperate to garner engagement, likes and shares of their carefully integrated ads, they even pay 'influencers' with large followings thousands of dollars to promote their products for the exact same reason.

Likeability

We all know that we are generally attracted to a certain set of people that we consider likable. This extends to friends and family members across the board. So in order to get others to like you and in turn be open to persuasion by you, you must first transition into a friend or acquaintance. This ties in closely with the reciprocity principle and here are some basic steps to follow for the same result.

- The first step will be the attraction phase. You will have to give a person something that they will be instantly drawn to.

- Make it relatable. People will be drawn to you if you are in turn relatable to them. You will find it easier to influence someone if they consider you their friend.

- It will be vital to communicate as a friend. You will have to make use of good communication skills to get into their good books.

- Make it look like you are in the same group as them and fighting for the same causes. This will help increase rapport.

Authority

If you wish to influence someone then you must dress and act the part. This means that you wear clothes and accessories that help you look like you are in command. Although this might seem quite superficial, it will only help you achieve your end goal. Here are some of the criteria to bear in mind.

- Wear clothes that are befitting of people's perception of authoritative figures within their life.

- Communicate to them in a direct commanding fashion.

- Make sure you learn the language and lexicon of the experts in that field. Talk how they talk.

There are many studies that have also confirmed this authority principle and none more so than the famous Milgram obedience experiments. These studies were conducted at Yale University by psychologist Stanley Milgram in 1963, where an experimenter instructed a teacher to ask questions to a learner (actor). The teacher was instructed to pass increasingly greater electric shocks to the learner if he failed to answer a question correctly. The learner was instructed to give away wrong answers and act like he was in pain when the fake shock was administered.

The researchers were surprised to find that the teacher would continue to pass the electric shock to the learner, sometimes with even the highest voltage just because the experimenter would ask him to despite not hearing a response from the learner, who was now asked to be silent. This illustrated that the teacher would simply follow instructions from the experimenter even when they believed they were delivering a potentially lethal shock just because someone of authority in a white coat was telling them to do so.

The findings of these experiments were later cited at many German Nazi war criminal hearings taking into consideration that the thousands of Germans complicit in the concentration camps of the holocaust were simply following orders from extremely authoritative figures.

Scarcity

The last "weapon" of influence of the 6 is the principle of scarcity. Human beings like exclusivity and are drawn to things that they will not find anywhere else. By making something exclusive you will have the chance to enhance its value. They are also fearful when something they desire starts to disappear. It's your classic supply and demand principle, if something is abundant than it will have a perceived lower value and be cheap, if it is rare then it will have high value and be expensive.

This works for products and human beings in exactly the same way. Here are some aspects to bear in mind.

- Always imply that whatever you are offering (whether it is something physical or information) is not available anywhere else.

- Try to implement a countdown timer on whatever you are offering so there is a clear indication of when it will disappear.

- Never go back on the original stipulations I mentioned above. It's critical to show people that what you offered them was indeed genuinely scarce to ensure the effectiveness of this method in future instances.

Any of that seem familiar? It should do if you suspect someone is manipulating you. There is a fine line between honest persuasion and manipulation and as I mentioned above, the lines can get blurred very easily.

So make sure you go back and study these principles a number of times. I have certainly seen them working in the real world with my consulting business with clients, prospects and employees alike. But most importantly so you can get a feel for when a manipulative person is using them against you.

CHAPTER 8

DEALING WITH MANIPULATION IN A RELATIONSHIP

"The moment you feel like you need to prove yourself, is the moment you need to be silent and walk away"

(Rachel Wolchin)

As I have mentioned previously, everyone is vulnerable to being manipulated at some stage in their life – whether that's within the relationships with parents, spouse or romantic partner, children, friends, co-workers, bosses, or neighbors. The moment you allow another person to manipulate you, you are colluding with their desire to take control over your feelings, thoughts, and motives through exploitative, unfair, and deceptive means.

All manipulative relationships are unbalanced and one-sided. Only the manipulator benefits from these kinds of relationships for the most part. In this chapter, I will give you the basic tips on how to deal with this type of situation if it does arise in your life.

Know Your Rights

Above all, *you should know your basic rights and know when they are being violated.* For as long as you are not the one causing harm to others, you have the right to defend these rights and stand up for yourself. But if you bring harm to others, you automatically forfeit these rights.

You have the right to:

- Express your own opinions, wants, and feelings.

- Have your own set of beliefs and opinions that are different from other people.

- Be treated with utmost respect.

- Say *no* without guilt.

- Set your own priorities.

- Be compensated for what you pay for.

- Care for and protect yourself from physical, mental, and emotional threats.

- Most importantly live a happy and healthy life in general.

Emotional and psychological manipulators have no regard for these rights. However, *you have the moral authority and the power to declare that it is you, alone, who can change your life.*

Stay Away

You have been given tips in earlier chapters on how to detect a manipulator even from a distance. Keep in mind that a manipulator acts with different faces with different people and situations. They easily adapt to people and their situations.

Most skilled manipulators tend to be highly polite to others, and rude to another. They can appear helpless one minute, and suddenly become aggressive the next.

Once you observe these behaviors in someone, *do not engage with that person, unless there is no other choice.* Do not make it your life's mission to change them, being a manipulative individual is deep-seated. By all means try to highlight this behavior in a loved one but other peripheral people in your life, your best bet is avoidance, you cannot change them and it's nit your duty to do so.

Do not Resort to Self-Blame

You've learned that manipulators exploit your weaknesses. They will make you feel inadequate, to the point of blaming yourself for not giving them what they want. Keep in mind that *you are not the problem, so you shouldn't feel bad about yourself.*

Ask yourself these questions:

- *Am I treated with respect?*

- *Are we in a give-and-take kind of relationship?*

- *Are their demands and expectations of me reasonable?*

- *Essentially, am I still happy being in this relationship?*

Your answers should give you clues if you are still in a healthy relationship or not.

Ask More Probing Questions

It is expected that manipulative individuals will make demands of you – which will often make you do things out of your comfort zone just to meet their needs. When they make unreasonable requests, it's important to ask them back some questions, rather than immediately giving in to their requests.

- *Do I have a say in this request?*

- *Does this sound reasonable to you?*

- *Are you making a request or making a demand?*

- *Do you think this is fair?*

- *What is in it for me?*

- *Do you really expect me to (state the unreasonable request)?*

Be firm. You are unmasking the true intentions of a manipulator, if they have some degree of self-awareness, they will immediately back down. But, pathological manipulators will simply find ways to dismiss your questions and insist on granting their request.

Take Advantage of Time

Aside from asking for unreasonable requests, manipulators want to get answers right away. Don't give in to pressure and don't allow them to control you, hence rather than responding immediately, leverage on time and tell them you'll think about it. Take your time to analyze the situation, its pros and cons. Consider also, if you want to negotiate or you'll simply say *no* to the request.

Firmly Say *No* – Albeit, Diplomatically

If you can give a firm and diplomatic "no" is to practice the ultimate art of communication. When effectively articulating you reasons for not wanting to do something, you appear to stand your ground while keeping a workable relationship.

Go back to the fundamental rights – it is your right to set your own priorities, and you have the right to say *no* without guilt. If there is one thing that I see in easily manipulated people (myself included at one stage) is that they say yes to every request way to fast and way to often.

Fight Back Bullies

Fight back but stay safe. Skilled manipulators can become extremely intimidating. Don't let them see you as weaker than them. Many bullies are cowards inside. The moment their targets stand up to them, bullies will more often than not back down. They don't want confrontations. The irony is that they are actually weak, especially when their targets fight back.

But make sure that when you do fight back, you can protect yourself, like having other people with you to support and be a witness. When things get physical and abusive, it's time to consult the police and a lawyer. It's one thing to stand up to bullies, it's another thing to be wise and not do it on your own.

Learn to Set Consequences

When a manipulator continues to insist on trampling on your boundaries, and won't accept your answer of "no", set some consequences for that behavior.

Learn to identify and assert consequences. When well-articulated, these consequences will cause the manipulator to *pause and swing from violation to respect.*

The key to dealing with manipulative individuals is learning how to be assertive in protecting your basic human rights. Everything starts and ends with your rights – if people begin to walk all over you, it's the perfect time to fight back and reclaim your control over your own life.

CHAPTER 9

HOW TO RAISE YOUR OVERALL SELF-ESTEEM

If there is one true antidote to manipulating behavior and shielding yourself from it, it is this - raising your overall self-esteem and self-worth. It protects you in a way that's not immediately obvious, but extremely powerful none the less.

It's not some clever tactic to employ to deflect negative comments or anything like that, but rather raising you own self-confidence which no longer makes you are target. It inoculates yourself from ever being subjected to manipulative behavior in the first place as it is usually directed towards someone in a moment of transition or temporary vulnerability.

No one can control you and manipulate you if you have high regard for yourself. In truth nothing is more important than how you think and feel about yourself, that goes for manipulation and life/success in general.

Handle Your Inner Critic.

You have an inner critic, everyone does. Listening to your inner critic helps you get things done or helps you do things that will gain acceptance from other people. The inner voices can also kill your self-esteem if you let it.

I have described the importance of separating the "thinker" from the "feeler" within you in previous books. Needless to say that over thinking situations is not a good thing to do, I would go as far as to say its the biggest plight on civilization today.

It is normal for you inner voice to suggest both positive and negative thoughts. It's not about blocking out the noise and analyzing what you are thinking, and if it is of any benefit to you? If it isn't, then it's about preventing yourself from going down the rabbit hole of negative and spiraling imaginary scenarios.

Refocus those negative thoughts into something constructive and happier.

Cultivate a Gratitude Mindset

Learn to appreciate yourself, and all of the good things about your life. When you feel good about yourself and grateful for the things that you do have, your mind won't have room to entertain negative thoughts.

Most of the suffering people have in their lives is imaginary. It's created from the dissonance between where they are and where they think they would like to be. But that is a false horizon, if you can't be happy with the journey then you will never be content with wherever you are heading as there will always be the next thing.

The trick is to be happy now, I know it sounds over simplified and easier said then done, but it really is the one thing which gave me the most joy in life when I was struggling with my business in the early days.

It has been showed that the top business people in the world do this (and all successful people in general). If they are currently at point 'B' in their lives, they do not look forward to point 'C' and say "look how far I have to go." As I mentioned previously, this is just a conceptual place like the horizon of the earth. Every time you try to chase after it, it disappears further into the distance.

Instead what these people do is look back at point 'A' to where they started and say "hey, look how far I have come!" This is a subtle change of outlook but I promise you, if you do make this one adjustment in your thinking your whole outlook on life will change, and for the better. You will instantly start feeling grateful and satisfied with your current lot and much less frustrated with not yet being where you think you should be.

Put Things Into Writing

You can also write down the things that you like about yourself in a journal, the positive traits you have and situations they affects.

When you are feeling low, or when the day is not turning out well for you, or when negative thoughts begin to creep into your subconscious, take out your list and reread them. You can update them daily, or when you discover something new and positive about yourself.

It's a good idea to start your day with going over these statements as they work a little like affirmations. You are cultivating the positive emotions surrounding these attributes or events and allowing you to feel them again in the here and now. Remember the brain has no way of telling the difference with regards to emotions I.e. the event could be happening now, 10 years ago or some way into the future!

Stop Being a Perfectionist

Aiming to be perfect all the time can be very destructive. Just like negative thoughts, perfectionism can paralyze you from getting things done because of your fear of not living up to a high standard you have set for yourself. This may also result in procrastination, thus, ending up not getting you the results you expected. This will bring your self-esteem crashing down if you let it.

Try making these alterations to your thinking to overcome perfectionism:

- *Strive for good enough.* Stop aiming for perfection, remember nobody's perfect. When you aim for perfection all the time, you won't finish any task because you'll either wait for the right time or continue to work on it until it turns out perfect (which will never happen).

- *Striving for perfection will only hurt you in the long run.* Remind yourself that life is not a fairy tale that always ends with *a happily ever after.* Learn to manage your expectations, because after all, this is real life. You have managed to deal with everything life has thrown at you up until this point, how do I know this? Because you are still alive reading this today. The true curve balls in life you will never see coming so there is absolutely no point in worrying about them today. You will deal with them at the time as you always have done, so stop worrying.

Look at Mistakes and Failure as Lessons

It is inevitable that you will make mistakes from time to time. You will fail on some days. But the good thing about experiencing failures and committing mistakes is that there are lessons to be learnt from them all.

There will always be something positive you can take out of every situation, you just have to find what they are. Learn from it and internalize it and come back stronger. "You either win or you learn" as they say. I couldn't agree more.

Similar to this, you always need to be trying something new. Get out of your comfort zone as much and as often as possible. That is the only true route to feeling content and successful in life. In having new experiences and learning new things that will feed into your positive confidence and self-esteem feedback loops.

They do not need to be big and scary all of the time, just small wins, increment progress will do the job. As long as you are moving in the right direction, that is all that counts.

Stop Comparing Yourself to Others

You will never be good enough if you keep on comparing yourself with other people. You will never win because there's always someone better or there is always something better to attain out there. You are only ever in a competition with yourself, to improve on the version of you from yesterday or a year ago.

Remember to always look back at 'A', not forward to 'C'. Look at how far you have come as person with regards to your development. Other people are on their own journey, let them get on with it. Only you walk in your shoes, be proud of that and keep walking your own path.

Be Around People who are Supportive of You

This is fairly obvious but most people still do not take as much notice of this concept as they should. It's simple, don't hang around negative people who only sees the things that you have done wrong. This includes the manipulators!

Try to be around positive people, those who are willing to support you and lift you up. This is easier said then done regarding close friends and family but you do have to draw the line somewhere. Be with people who will pick you up when you fall and help you get back on our feet again.

There is a saying in business that "Your network is your net worth" or that you are the sum of the five people you most commonly spend time with. So make sure these people are positive in nature and have an uplifting effect on you and not the opposite. It can make all the difference in your life.

SUMMARY

The concept of manipulation is no doubt a controversial one as it effects us in the most personal and intimate way, often with people we care about the most. However it is still very important to be able to recognize when this type of behavior is occurring in your life.

Essentially there are two types of behavior, overt (outward, obvious and aggressive) and covert (subtle, quiet and deceptive) when it comes to manipulation. Both are awful to experience in their own right however it is the covert version which is so prevalent in society and can be very difficult to spot.

It's wise to first step back and recognize why people do the things they do, what are their motives and drives? Whilst humans share very similar needs and desires in a base sense, such as shelter, food, love, compassion and freedom from violence as Maslow's Pyramid shows us. However it's when people have met these basic needs do they sometimes go awry.

A manipulators motives are inherently selfish and are almost always a result of insecurity and a low level of consciousness themselves other wise they wouldn't behave they way they do. These people aren't necessarily bad people, maybe they are just going through some difficult times themselves. As I suggested in the opening remarks to this book, people often behave this way earlier on in life.

However its the people who hold onto these tendencies into adult life who can be the most hurtful and dangerous. That is who I'm referring to most when I write about the strategies to defend against manipulation, and it starts with assessing why and who they are likely to target the most.

It's usually people who are in some form of transition, they are going through a big career or housing move for example. They may not be as cognizant of what is going on around them and too preoccupied with what they are doing. It may also be that you have suffered a recent loss and are also in somewhat of a disarray and looking for something to comfort you and fill the gap.

Commonly targeted people are also usually insecure in nature who experience high levels of fear and anxiety themselves. They are also very trusting and quick to forgive, they are "too nice". All of the personality traits that endear them to other caring folk leaves them vulnerable and open to less honorable and deceptive people.

However you are always in control of your situation if you think so or not. It's simply about improving your verbal and non-verbal communication skills to better pick up on these manipulative signals when they arise. It's also about articulating your own thoughts and feelings to leave no room for misunderstanding when it comes to discussing every relationship in your life.

CONCLUSION

"Nobody can hurt me without my permission"

(Mahatma Gandhi)

Manipulation is really not a trivial thing and it can destroy peoples relationships and lives if its left to continue. If you have been affected by this type of behavior (which I imagine a high percentage of people reading this will have) than you know how tough it can be. Just know that there is light at the end of the tunnel and it always starts with you.

In reality this whole process boils down to one thing, manipulation only happens if you let it. Yes you may unexpectedly get taken down the wrong path to begin with, but after a while you know what is happening even if it's subconsciously.

However after that it's up to you what you do, when you are consciously aware what is going on you have a choice to either stand and take it or not. I know that may sound like an over simplification but it really is that straight forward. I also know that it may not be that easy as it's sometimes people you care about who are indulging in this type of behavior against either yourself of others.

But truthfully there is simply no reason or excuse for manipulative behavior in any circumstance in adult life. Nothing needs to be deceitful and hidden from view in a grown up conversation and relationship. The world is a big enough place to move on from any ill will or miss understanding.

Everyone makes mistakes from time to time and that's OK. But the key is to be honest about it, try to fix wrong doings you have made and move on. If a person is unhappy within a relationship the solution is always openness and honesty.

It's not selfish to lead a happy and fulfilling life, it's your basic right! Everyone around you benefits from you being happy as you are more likely to uplift others, guide them, give financial support, it helps in respect to just about every aspect you can think of.

The best thing you can honestly do is set a good example, be the light, the best version of yourself and in tern the people who are able to change will take notice and rectify their own behavior if they so choose.

Hopefully I have given you some pointers and observations on how to do just that, how to deal with manipulation within your life a little better. So go ahead and put some of these strategies into place today!

I wish you love and the very best of luck.

BONUS CHAPTER

(From 'Emotional Intelligence: A Psychologist's Guide')

CHAPTER 4

TAKING INVENTORY OF YOUR EMOTIONAL STATE

"Educating the mind without educating the heart is
no education at all"

(Aristotle)

One of the most important things you can do when initially starting out on your emotional intelligence enhancing journey is to take stock of what you are currently feeling. There is no right or wrong answers here in terms of what come up. As our limbic legacy show us, humans are inherently emotional creatures and suppressing them is almost impossible to do entirely.

However you do have control over the way you react to these tendencies, the thoughts and behaviors after the fact. The following factors should help you take a closer look into how to identify and deal with these feelings when they do arise to ultimately move you to the next level in your E.Q. journey.

Acknowledge Your Emotions

The first thing to do when attempting to increase your personal E.Q. levels is to get good at acknowledging and perceiving the emotions that you are feeling. This is the starting point for every model and framework of E.Q.

Whenever I feel an emotion arise within me I always take a pause and acknowledge its presence, I take a moment and really feel it so I can understand and label it in my mind. This isn't the same as reacting or acting upon the emotion just yet, but I want to know why it may have arisen and if it could be useful to me. If it's a feeling of anger, fear or frustration I do not deny or try to hide it, but instead acknowledge its presence and dismiss it as not being productive and move on.

If you start to dwell on emotions such as these you will quickly fall into a negative spiral thought process that will have you framing everything in a pessimistic light before you know it. I used to play out entire imaginary scenarios in my head of something going badly and the knock-on effects that I 'knew' it would have, only to realize that it NEVER worked out that badly and that I'd fabricated it all in my mind. Sound familiar?

If on the other hand it is an emotion of excitement, joy or anticipation, I also pause for a moment, acknowledge and label what it is that I'm feeling and try to cultivate and utilize it if I think it will benefit the situation such as situational empathy (which we will get onto later).

It is also important to take responsibility for these emotions that you are feeling either way, good or bad. Know that it is something inside of you which is eliciting such a response and that you have to deal with it and not sweep it under the carpet so to speak. This is usually the most challenging step for people, but it is also the most rewarding. Yes it maybe some outside influence or stimulus that sparked the response in the first place, but remember that the emotions you are feeling are coming from within you and that it's your responsibility to deal with them

Understand That You Are Not Your Emotions

So following on from that, you also need to constantly remind yourself that the emotions which arise within you and the conscious entity which interprets them are two very different things. Most people walk around in somewhat of a waking sleep for the most part completely at the mercy of any feeling, thought or emotion that pops into their head.

You have to understand that many thoughts and emotions will pass through you almost on a second by second basis, but again it's entirely your choice on how you perceive and choose to react to them.

There is also a very large egoic element to this process as well. Thoughts and feelings of jealously for another person or fear of performing a task is really just your ego trying to keep your preconceived notions about the world intact and keep you operating within your comfort zone. This is a topic for much greater discussion i.e. regarding the tactics to counteract such self-sabotaging behavior, but needless to say that detaching yourself from your overall emotional state is very a beneficial thing to do.

Learn to Forgive Yourself & Others

"Life becomes easier when you learn to accept an apology you never got"

(Robert Brault)

Again, along the same lines as letting go of a negative emotion that arises within you, people have a great tendency to hold onto what they perceive to be negative acts that they have either committed themselves or others against them. Holding onto this ill feeling again serves absolutely no purpose to you in the immediate future and certainly not the long run. *"Holding onto anger is like drinking poison and expecting the other person to die"* as the Buddha so aptly put it.

If there was one thing that got me ahead in my business life so quickly it was this concept. Once I stopped getting caught up with what I thought I deserved from a situation or others around me and started pushing ahead regardless, I made so much more progress. You can't stop and throw stones at every dog that barks, and that includes yourself when you mess up.

This isn't just applicable to adult and business life either, it's relates to everyone young or old. If I had taken heed of this advice when I was growing up I know I would have had better overall relationships with school/college friends and family alike. That's not to say things were necessarily that bad, but they could have been better, or at least I could have saved myself a great deal of heart ache and stress in the along the way.

Don't Get Involved in Negative Self-Talk

As I mentioned above, letting negative self talk get out of hand is a very bad habit to take up. I would say that it is the one thing that plagues humanity more than anything. We often talk ourselves out of things before we've had a chance to start them. Again this comes down to letting negative thoughts and emotions cloud our thinking to a point of almost no escape. You have to stop this in its tracks as quickly as possible if you want to build high overall levels of emotional intelligence.

This also includes negative self-talk and 'gossip' regarding other people. In danger of sounding like one of your parents or school teacher here, you don't need me to tell you this is a worthless exercise and one that will ultimately bring your E.Q. level down with it. No one is perfect; just make a point of catching yourself when you start to talk in this way.

Also along the same lines as the above, you must try and do your best not to judge others where ever possible. This actually freed me greatly in a psychological sense when I managed to stop doing it a few years ago. I never thought of myself as an overly judgmental person but I still realized I would do it from time to time. But stopping myself altogether from judging anyone I came across in even the smallest way saves me so much mental energy and almost certain daily miss judgment.

Nowadays I simply let others go about their day in their own way without even the slightest judging thought about their behavior. That is not to say that I tolerate bad behavior or that I do not try and empathize with people and attempt to understand their situation better, which is critical to building fruitful relationships. But I don't judge them with regards to how they got to where they are, I never walked in their shoes or went through the struggles they did so I let them do the talking on this one.

Again this isn't some "holier than thou" situation, I'm not perfect and do very occasionally catch myself automatically judging someone. I just now catch it very early and stop myself in my tracks straight away. It's so much more liberating when you do.

BONUS CHAPTER

(From 'NLP: A Psychologist's Guide')

CHAPTER 6

FRAMING TECHNIQUES

"If you don't like something, change it. If you cannot change it, change the way you think about it"

(Madras Proverb)

Framing techniques within NLP usually fit in well with many other strategies. Framing complements just about everything in the way it can amplify or deamplify emotional states by rebuilding pathways within the primal limbic region of the brain, more specifically between the amygdala and hippocampus.

Before I dive into the specifics of applying the framing techniques it's wise to identify what we are dealing with in terms of "frames of reference" from an emotional stand point. Humans tend to learn lessons and ascribe meaning to things due to the events surrounding that situation. More specifically the memories we have regarding them.

If you think about it, both your life's past memories and future projections are nothing more than a show real, a filmstrip much like the negatives you see on those old movie projectors. They are just snapshots of events that we attribute meaning too after the fact. However what people don't usually realize is that meaning or emotional connection you may have related to something may not be accurate and can be changed.

You've heard of the saying "If it's true for you, then it's true". That is a suggestion of projection of reality into the world and is more of an observation within quantum mechanics. But it couldn't be more true in an experiential sense, especially when it comes to feelings and emotions. What is happening in your brain is the hippocampus is storing this long term memory data whilst another part, the amygdala is producing the emotion associated with it.

Although very close together anatomically, these two regions still need to communicate to produce the complete picture of the event with the emotions/meanings also attached. Sometimes they get this wrong, or you can certainly alter this association if you do not like what you see, or more accurately, what you feel.

Framing Negative Emotions

I believe the best place to start with framing is to remove or deamplify negative connotations to events which is what holds people back the most in my opinion, it certainly was the case for me. Similar to collapsing a negative anchor, start by thinking of a time that you perceived something to have gone badly, something that didn't turn out well and you now have a negative outlook on. This might be failing your driving test or an interview that didn't go well.

What you have done is dig out one of these negative memories from your hippocampus within the limbic system, and it is now being displayed as a picture or short video reel within your prefrontal cortex, the rational part of the brain which is making sense of it. Additionally the amygdala will be asked for the emotional data and will provide it as such, this will be negative emotions of fear, anxiety or disappointment most likely. The amygdala also has no real sense of time so the emotions will feel fresh as if the event was happening again in the here and now.

Let's use the example of a failed driving test. I failed at my first attempt so can relate to this one personally. You may have prepared really well and done all of the turns perfectly with your instructor in the weeks leading up to the test. However on the day of test you arrived at the driving center late due to bad weather and heavy traffic, you were flustered and in a rush as a result. Certainly not in a nice and calm state ready to get on the road yourself.

Now form a picture of the event in your mind, make it one clear snapshot or frame that really sums up and encapsulates the moment. It might be you stalling the car on a hill start or sitting in the parking lot afterwards when feeling dejected. Whatever it is, form a picture of it.

Now try to step back from the situation, if you were looking at the picture through your own eyes then start to view it from a third person perspective looking down on the image from the corner of the frame. If you were already withdrawn from the image than take an even further step back and view it from an even greater detached position from say a little way down the street.

You should now be able to see yourself clearly in this picture, a frame that perfectly represents you failing your driving test that day. However what you want to do now is actually blur the image a little, make it grainy and black and white like an old film negative I was describing above. Also put a physical frame around it, something like an old fashioned stainless steel frame you see in grand mansions in movies. The picture should now be seen to have a different texture, a pastel paint look perhaps.

The next thing to do is put this picture up on the wall, this may be in an art gallery or large house, just someplace where people will glance at it before they move along with what they are doing without any real interest.

Finally start to think about that memory/image once more in your mind. I used the example of the failed driving test here as many can relate to that (but whatever it is for you just substitute it in).

What you should find is that the memory has noticeably decreased in negative emotion. It may still feel a little uncomfortable but nowhere near what it used to be. The trick is to go back and do this again with the same scenario, with that same image and any other images that may be linked to the memory. Put them all up on the wall beside one another and see how they no longer elicit the same emotions they once did. They are now simply old pictures on a wall.

Framing Positive Emotions

The previous advice on framing negative past situations should have helped you view past traumatic events in a much more neutral and objective light, robbing them of their emotional baggage and letting you move on with things in your life. However there are times when you want to do the reverse i.e. framing moments in a more positive manner. This simply means you will again be taking previous events and situations from your past but this time amplifying their meaning and effect they have on you.

This may be done for a number of reasons, say enhancing an old memory with friends and family for example. But for me this strategy was most helpful again in a self-development sense. I used it to heighten moments of brief success into much more elaborate light. Remember these situations have no intrinsic meanings in and of themselves, just the one's you decide to give them

For me it was about anchoring and triggering more positive emotions onto milestones that I had made in my business life to fuel further progress and to feed into my positive feedback loops to greater snowball my success into the future. That is what is great about your life, you can use NLP techniques such as these to completely design and direct it in any direction your like. It just takes learning a few skills and techniques such as these in order to do so.

So back to the positive framing strategy. When you are attempting to prepare yourself for an important or upcoming event such as an interview, business meeting and the like, you first need to imagine yourself in a plain and empty room. Then ask yourself "In what way would I like the people in this up coming event to view me?" How would you like others to look at you and see you as a person?

The image you have in your head will be the image you are starting to construct here, don't force it just start to build the situation, your movements and body language and how you see yourself acting in general. Everything from the way you are facing to the clothes you are wearing.

Now watch the picture unfold as the situation is going extremely well, you are confidently conducting the meeting. People are really enjoying and appreciating the way you are delivering what you are saying and may even be giving you light applause and congratulations. Watch how you confidently accept the adulation with a smile and a straight back.

Now it is about putting this powerful, confident and calm image into the situation and surroundings of the upcoming event/ meeting. Put yourself right there, see the visuals, the colors and textures of the room. Smell your favorite perfume or aftershave on yourself to further increase assurance. Be as vivid as possible with this, once again see yourself completely convincing everybody in the room with what you are saying. See them smiling and laughing at your jokes or whatever it is you need to achieve.

Now blow this image up to 100 feet in diameter and watch it on an LCD screen directly in front of you within the empty room. It's so large that it fills an entire wall! The next thing to do is to take a big stride into the picture, merge yourself with the digital image on the screen. Experience the situation through your own eyes, you are now thinking and feeling every sight, sound and emotion as if it were happening to you right here and now. Take as long as you like soaking in the feelings of the super confident and calm person . This is your true self-image.

Rehearse this as many times as you like and for as many situations as you want. You should start to automatically put yourself in the confidant persons shoes as it will feel so natural to you as you have now been there many times before. Again the mind doesn't know the difference between an imagined or "real" event. You are simply littering your future film reel with positive and success stories from an emotional standpoint. When you actually get there it will seem familiar and natural to behave in that way.

I sometimes like to go back in time to also do this process for negative events. I find it supplements the picture framing process I described above. I not only frame the situation I viewed as going badly into an outdated and irrelevant image, I also like to replay certain scenarios on my big screen and see it as going amazingly well. Do this enough and the mind soon builds those new neural pathways and starts to forgets or at least downplays the negative side and instead projects it in a positive light.

This isn't lying to yourself as such i.e. telling yourself that you made that deal when you didn't or passed the exam when you in fact failed it. As the process states, you are simply re-framing the event with regards to an emotional standpoint. You are just creating a new outlook on it, one which serves you better.

This can be done for any past or future situation you would like. It can be done for any perceived strength or weakness you might have i.e. amplify the positive one and downplay the negative. Inferring meaning is the key here, you have total control over that one. Nothing has any intrinsic meaning, only the one in which you give it.

www.ingramcontent.com/pod-product-compliance
Lightning Source LLC
Chambersburg PA
CBHW072059280526
45788CB00006B/2327